TEETH, TAILS, & TENTACLES

An Animal Counting Book

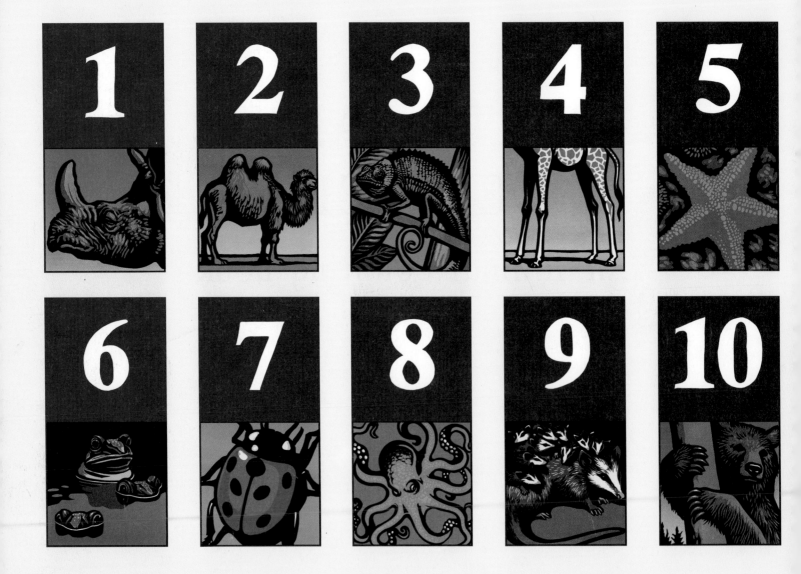

TEETH, TAILS, & TENTACLES

An Animal Counting Book

BY CHRISTOPHER WORMELL

SCHOLASTIC INC.

New York Toronto London Auckland Sydney Mexico City New Delhi Hong Kong Buenos Aires

I would like to thank Elizabeth Encarnacion, Buz Teacher, Frances Soo Ping Chow, Dustin Summers, and Andra Serlin for the original concept of this book, some great ideas for the pictures, and for putting the whole thing together and making it look so good.

ISBN 0-439-78428-X

12 11 10 9 8 7 6 5 4

14 15 16/0

40

Printed in the U.S.A.

First Scholastic printing, September 2005

Cover and interior design by Dustin Summers
Edited by Elizabeth Encarnacion
Typography: Caslon

To William

1

ONE

rhinoceros horn

2

TWO

camel humps

3

THREE

chameleon colors

FOUR

giraffe legs

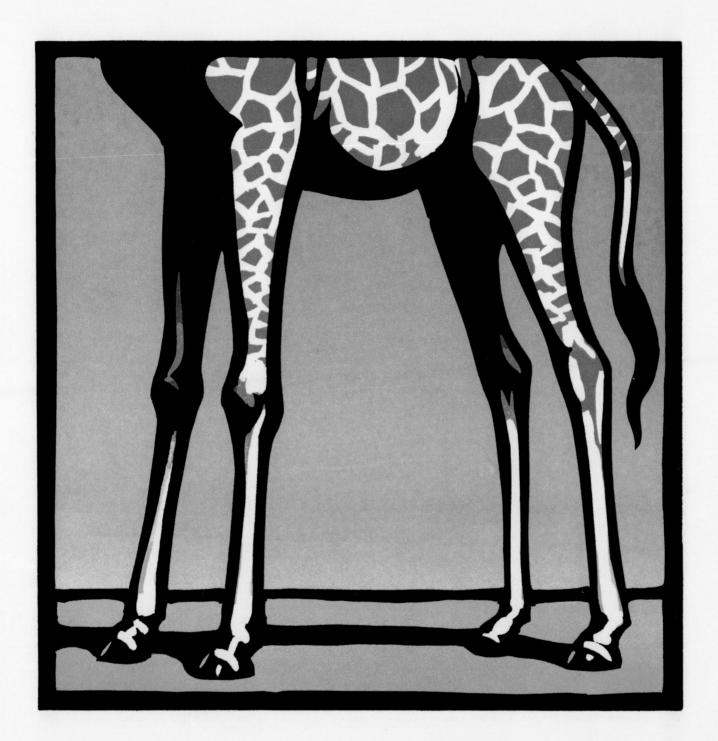

5

FIVE

starfish
arms

6
SIX

frog eyes

7

SEVEN

black spots on
a ladybug

EIGHT

octopus
tentacles

9

NINE

opossum
babies

10

TEN

bear claws

11
ELEVEN

goose eggs

12

TWELVE

antler points
on a stag

13

THIRTEEN

caterpillar segments

14

FOURTEEN

white rings
on a lemur

15

FIFTEEN

leopard
rosettes

16

SIXTEEN

catfish whiskers

17

SEVENTEEN

zebra stripes

18
EIGHTEEN

diamond markings
on a rattlesnake

19

NINETEEN

crocodile
teeth

20
TWENTY

barnacle shells
on . . .

1

ONE

humpback
whale

SPECIFIC ANIMALS FEATURED
IN THIS BOOK

INDIAN RHINOCEROS: A hairless, gray mammal that is now an endangered species only found naturally in preserves in India and Nepal. The Indian Rhinoceros has one sharp, ivory horn made from keratin, a protein also found in hair, and eats mainly grasses and shrubs.

BACTRIAN CAMEL: A furry, brown beast of burden that is native to the Gobi desert in Mongolia and has long eyelashes and nostrils that close to keep sand out of its eyes and nose. Bactrian camels have two humps that store fat, allowing the animal to go without food and water for long periods as the fat is converted into energy and water and the humps become smaller.

CHAMELEON: A lizard, found in parts of southern Europe, the Middle East, southwestern Asia, and Africa, with a long, sticky tongue that is used to catch insects. Chameleons are known for their ability to change colors in response to changes in light, temperature, or environment.

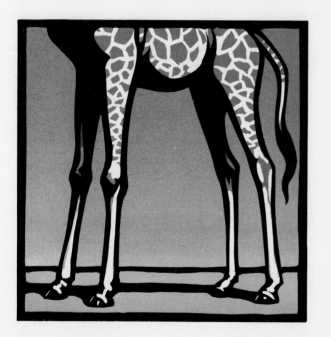

GIRAFFE: A plant-eating mammal with a long, muscular neck and a distinctive coat pattern that lives in the dry, open grasslands and woodlands south of the Sahara Desert in Africa. Giraffes have long and slender legs with heavy hooves that can injure an attacking animal, and they sometimes sleep standing upright.

OCHRE STARFISH: A sea-dwelling invertebrate with rough and leathery skin and a simple, brainless nervous system that is common to the beaches of western North America. Ochre starfish have five arms that will regenerate, or re-grow, when they are damaged or lost.

AMERICAN BULLFROG: A greenish-brown, aquatic amphibian named after the male's distinctive, resonant call, that lives in North America, the Caribbean islands, and Europe. The American bullfrog's powerful hind legs allow it to leap out of the water to catch insects, young birds, and even small mammals it spots above the surface with its large and bulging eyes.

SEVEN-SPOTTED LADYBUG: A small, round red beetle that eats aphids and is commonly found throughout the world in temperate regions. The seven-spotted ladybug has two hardened wing covers, made of a material similar to human finger-nails and marked with seven distinctive black spots, that protect thin, transparent wings.

OCTOPUS: A carnivorous marine mollusk with a well-developed brain that can shoot water jets to move quickly and releases ink when threatened. The octopus, found worldwide in tropical and warm temperate seas, has eight long tentacles, that bear two rows of suckers each and may be regenerated if damaged.

VIRGINIA OPOSSUM: A nocturnal marsupial with a long, pointed nose and a prehensile tail that lives primarily in woodland and grassland areas of the eastern United States. A female Virginia opossum carries its babies in an abdominal pouch for about two months until the young are developed enough to ride on its back for another four to six weeks.

BROWN BEAR: A large, furry mammal that eats both plants and animals and lives in the forests and treeless tundra of Europe, Asia, and North America. Brown bears may mark their territory by biting, rubbing, and clawing the bark of trees in their home range to communicate with other bears.

CANADA GOOSE: A migratory bird with a white chest and a long, black neck that is native to the marshes, rivers, ponds, lakes, and fields of North America. Canada geese mate for life, with the female building the nest and incubating the eggs, and the male helping to protect and care for the goslings after they hatch.

RED DEER STAG: A hoofed, plant-eating mammal with reddish-brown fur and a short tail that is found in Europe, Asia, and North America. The male red deer, called a stag, has large, branched antlers that are used to fight with other stags during mating season and are shed annually.

CINNABAR MOTH CATERPILLAR: The larval stage of the cinnabar moth, which has been introduced around the world to help control the noxious tansy ragwort weed. The caterpillar has black and yellow-orange bands that mark its segments, and grows rapidly for about a month before pupating in a cocoon for nine months and emerging as a cinnabar moth in the spring.

RING-TAILED LEMUR: A small, monkey-like mammal with a long, black and white striped tail that is native to Madagascar and eats fruits, leaves, and bark from plants. A male ring-tailed lemur may rub its scent onto its tail to spread the scent and assert dominance over another male.

CLOUDED LEOPARD: A large, feline carnivore that lives in the forests of southeast Asia and shares many characteristics with other large cats, but is not able to roar. The clouded leopard is an endangered species that is illegally hunted for its fur, which features brown-and-black-colored, cloud-shaped rosettes that provide camouflage to the animal in its environment.

BLUE CATFISH: A bluish-gray fish found in slow-moving rivers of the American Midwest and South that may grow to weigh as much as a hundred pounds. Catfish are named after the whisker-like barbels that extend from their jaws to help them sense food.

PLAINS ZEBRA: A striped, horse-like herbivore native to East Africa that has a short, spiky mane and a tufted tail. The black and white stripes of the plains zebra serve as protective coloration in its natural habitat and their unique patterns may help zebras recognize each other.

EASTERN DIAMONDBACK RATTLESNAKE: A poisonous snake, found in southeastern North America, that has a rattle on the end of its tail for warning off predators. The Eastern diamondback rattlesnake's diamond-shaped markings provide camouflage among the shrubs and grassy underbrush of its native habitat.

CROCODILE: A large, carnivorous reptile that lives in tropical waters throughout the world, including Africa, Asia, Australia, Central America, and southern Florida. Crocodiles have powerful jaws with interlocking teeth that are strong enough to crush the small mammals on which they feed.

BARNACLE: A small marine crustacean that attaches itself to whales, drifting wood, or man-made vessels in the Northern Atlantic Ocean and the North Sea and eats small particles of food as they drift along the ocean's currents.

HUMPBACK WHALE: A large, gray aquatic mammal that weighs about fifty-nine tons and may live up to ninety-five years. Humpback whales have baleen plates that separate and retain their food of krill and small fish as they expel sea water from their mouths.

Christopher Wormell is a leading English wood engraver. Inspired by the works of Thomas Bewick, he took up wood engraving in 1982, and has since illustrated several books in addition to his work in the fields of advertising, design, and editorial illustration.

Long before Christopher became a wood engraver he was taught lino-cutting by his father, mainly for the mass production of Christmas cards. Around Christmastime the Wormell household became something of a cottage industry with Christopher and his brothers and sisters producing handmade cards by the hundred.

His first book for children, *An Alphabet of Animals*, started as a series of simple, colorful lino-cut illustrations for his son Jack, and eventually grew into a book that took the Graphics Prize at the Bologna International Children's Book Fair in 1991. Some of Christopher's other children's book credits include *Mowgli's Brothers*, *Blue Rabbit and Friends*, *Blue Rabbit and the Runaway Wheel*, *Animal Train*, *Off to the Fair*, *George and the Dragon*, *Two Frogs*, *In the Woods*, *The Big Ugly Monster and the Little Stone Rabbit*, and *Swan Song*, a collection of poems by J. Patrick Lewis about extinct animals.

He lives in London with his wife and three children.

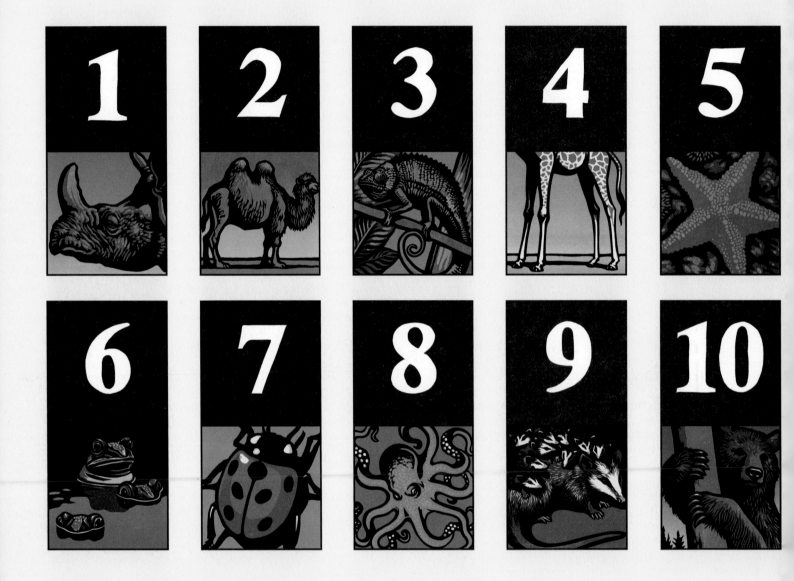